I0173210

Poetic Relief:
Yeah I Wrote It

By

TIKKIA

This book is dedicated to Francenia Tucker.
Rest in Peace my angel. Thanks for teaching
me to live, love, laugh and to go for it.

Table of Contents

Chapter 1: Feel Me On This
    1. My Offering..............................8
    2. She Can't Strut In My Pumps...11
    3. Lady Boss...........................13
    4. Silently Speaking.................15
    5. Full Disclosure....................17
    6. I'm On My Way.................19

Chapter 2: Stories Hold Facts Too
    1. Fairytales Are Forever...........21
    2. Reliving Reoccurring Rainy
       Days...............................23
    3. Cold Dark Room...................26
    4. The Middle of a Love Story.....30
    5. His Hip Hop......................34
    6. How It Seems.....................38

Chapter 3: Archetypes of Love
    1. A Mother's Love.................43
    2. Space.............................46
    3. You Make Me Feel.............48
    4. Your Kiss........................50
    5. Best Enemy......................52
    6. Falling...........................55
    7. This Can't Be Love.............57

Chapter 4: This Chapter's About Sex
1. Last Night...........................62
2. Made The First Move...........68
3. Heat Wave.........................70
4. Success Sex........................73
5. Good Morning....................74

Chapter 5: This Here Life
1. Life's Pleasures..................76
2. Just Blow It In The Sky.........79
3. Scars and Stripes................81
4. Tomorrow.........................84
5. Elements..........................86
6. That Kind of Fun................89

Chapter 6: Ruthless Undomesticated Heart
1. It Costs.....................................91
2. Feeling Some Kind of Way.....97
3. It's Complicated...................98
4. He Thinks I'm Sexy..............100
5. I Don't Love You................101
6. Over Before It Began...........102
7. No White Horse..................104

Chapter 1

Feel Me On This

**My Offering / She Can't Strut In My Pumps
Lady Boss / Silently Speaking / Full
Disclosure/ I'm On My Way**

My Offering

I offer you peace, honesty, confidence, love,
Pride, anxiety, fear, sadness, content,
Comfort, honor, lust, joy, grief, sex, humor,
Nonchalance, dreams, victory
 I offer you Poetic Relief.

Allow me to lie you down and whisper
Sweet verbs in your ear
As I massage your organ of intelligence
Relieving you of any fear.
Relax with me, read me, hear me, feel me
As I take you places you couldn't fathom
Making it so intense
Your eyes and your brain has
Simultaneous orgasms.
Put your feet up.
Lay your head back.
I want you to relax.
Feel the words as they cross the page
Appreciate the cadence and
The emotion displayed.

Memories you keep stored
In the back of your mind
Will resurface and affect you one last time.

Old friends, past loves and loves lost
Betrayal will try to haunt you at all costs.
Your accomplishments will come back
To congratulate you
And give you a pat on the back
To encourage you to move forward
And thank you for looking back

You will experience victory
As well as the agony of defeat
From past battles won and lost
For things which you were willing to
compete.
There will be times when you are
Completely at peace
With the world and with yourself
No longer feeling bound by a leash.

Freedom will become
A part of your natural life,
Taking what you want,
And sharing a big bite.
You will lust over new attractions.
You will become a bit more bold.
You will fall in love over and over again
The feeling will never get old.
You will laugh, you'll cry, get upset

Even experience a little scare
Then you'll remember a time
When you hadn't a care
And when you finish reading,
All of those feelings will still be there.
I offer you…Poetic Relief

She Can't Strut In My Pumps

She's tall and thin with long pretty hair
And her head is full
Of nothing but air.
She can't strut in my pumps.
She has a gorgeous smile and
A real nice style
And she does exercise…
Her mouth, running it for miles and miles.
She can't strut in my pumps.
She has fair skin and captivating eyes
One's so transparent
You can see through her innocent disguise.
She can't strut in my pumps.
She has an embrace that gives you
A little taste of comfort,
And a kiss that gives you butterflies,
And when she speaks
She gives you absolutely no insight.
She can't strut in my pumps.

I'm short, petit with a look that I own
I attract you with my benevolence and
Intrigue you with my intelligence.
She can't strut in my pumps.
Whether I'm in sneakers or stilettos

You can't take your eyes off of me
And you can look in my eyes to get a story.
She can't strut in my pumps.
The natural hollow on each side of my face
Form when I smile and it drives you wild
And you can't function properly
Without my witty style.
She can't strut in my pumps.
When we hold hands
Warmth runs through your soul
And when we part you clench your fist
To keep the feeling of my hand in your hold.
You like my devotion and
The authenticity I embody
Capturing your attention
Making you want to know me.
She can't strut in my pumps.
I have an embrace
That is the epitome of ease
And a kiss that makes you
Weak in the knees.
I mean
Isn't that exactly what you want?
She can't strut in my pumps.

Lady Boss

Sweat pants, high heels, glitter and unruly
hair.
Red lipstick 'cause I don't care
Large earrings you need a pair.
They say I think I'm cute.
They think I'm too sassy.
They mad their man want me.
They say I'm just hood classy.
Fuck 'em
I'm a lady boss. I'm a lady boss. I'm a lady
boss. I'm a lady boss.

Big hair, tattoos, ripped up jeans, and lip
gloss.
Fresh sneakers I like to floss
Old t-shirts I thought I lost.
They think
I should dress like them
They think I look bummy
That's 'til their man
Throw me all their cash
Then they don't think it's funny.
Fuck em
I'm a lady boss I'm a lady boss I'm a lady
boss I'm a lady boss

Business suit, tamed hair, but not my heels
Too high in the air
Diamond studs, brief case, platinum watch
I'm never late
I'm a lady boss I'm a lady boss I'm a lady
boss I'm a lady boss
They think I'm kinda mean.
They think I'm a little rude.
They don't like me delegating
Telling them what to do
They're confused 'cause
I'm a lady boss I'm a lady boss I'm a lady
boss I'm a lady boss

Silently Speaking

With shoes that scream the days greeting
I stand tall.

A smile on my face
You know it's going to be a good day.

My familiar face
They don't ask me my name
But they know it.

When I walk they follow me
They're looking for answers
I didn't get here
Shaking hands and kissing babies
But dropping the only jewels
Free to ladies.

With the aura of a queen
They can't help but follow me
And without fear
Because they know
This package is bigger than it appears.

My silence allows my words to last longer
Right now I don't have any

Or it could be that I have way too many to
speak
But you heard me

Full Disclosure

My hair defies gravity
Unless I instruct it otherwise
And my skin absorbs sunlight
Follow me
Make way
I give life

All of the perks of a woman
No stereotypical downfall
I stand sexy
I stand tall.
Capable of compassion but
Nobody cares about your feelings
But your mother.

I walk light
No burdens in sight.
I don't walk in circles
I have tunnel vision.
I don't think like a man,
But a woman with full hands.
I don't beat around the bush
I either sculpt it
Or cut it down.
Standing tall

I don't sit on my wisdom.

Feeling too heavy
I shed dead weight.
Hate is my nourishment
I'm fit.
You reap what you sow,
I'm flourishing.

I don't say much
It gets me in trouble
But never gets me out of it.
Not made of sugar, spice and everything nice
I'm savory
I might be trouble
You'll want to be served twice.

I'm On My Way

Racing after victory, I run
Full speed ahead, I run
I don't look back
It may slow me down
And I really don't need that right now.
I have to meet me there
I can't keep me waiting
Slowing only to a speed walk
When my legs start aching
I'm on my way

Chapter 2

Stories Hold Facts Too

*Fairytales Are Forever / Reliving
Reoccurring Rainy Days / Cold Dark Room
/ The Middle of a Love Story / His Hip Hop
/ How It Seems*

Fairytales are Forever

Soon to be crowned King
He desperately searched for
She who would be his Queen.
She who was of impeccable quality.
She who could appreciate even the little
things.
He searched for his beauty
For the one he couldn't live without
She wasn't easy to find
She wasn't to be found just wandering
Out and about.
He imagined that she would have long
flowing hair
And soft, beautiful legs that no one had ever
seen bare.
She would have a dimple in her chin
And she would have silky smooth skin.
She would have eyes
That would make him just
Want to fall inside.
She would have a laugh so sweet
It would make him weak.
He imagined her smile
Would drive him wild
For her he's been traveling miles and miles.

He searched high and low
For she who would follow him
Wherever he may go.
She would smell of lavender
And taste like honey
The best to be by his side
Together they would get money
They would fall in love, get married,
And even bear children
But he kept up his frantic search for her
…until then

Reliving Reoccurring Rainy Days

He dreads going to sleep
Because he dreads waking up
He knows that absolutely nothing has
changed
And it pisses him off because
He's reliving reoccurring rainy days.

He can't understand why he just can't get to
tomorrow.
He's not thinking about what he didn't take
from today.
He's just trying to proceed
Not considering the steps he needs follow.
He's not trying to hear
Slow down young man and take your time.
He already knows what he wants to do.
He's already made up his mind.

With open eyes and closed ears
The young man sets out
For success and overcoming his fears.
He wants so badly to live out his dreams.
He wants to do it all on his own.
But he's not prepared for what that really
means.

He knows with his whole heart
That he'll come out on top.
If he could only figure out
How to get out from under his own rock.
Unable to get to tomorrow he's
Reliving reoccurring rainy days.

He refuses to sleep
Because he's already awake
Trying to think of new ways to escape
He is reliving reoccurring rainy days.

His success is so close
That the young man can taste it.
Trying to figure out what he's missing
That just won't let him make it.
He's as thirsty as ever to succeed
To make those before him proud
And to help those after him
Live out their dreams.

Showing everyone that
You can dream without sleep
He never stops moving and
He never misses a beat
And with success on his mind
He refuses to face defeat.

Giving it his all
Without being given so much as a breeze
He's appreciative of the difficulty
For he knows that nothing good comes with
ease.
He knows that his efforts are not done in
vain,
Therefore he pushes even harder
To escape the rain.
But he still can't seem to get past this phase
And he's continuously
Reliving reoccurring rainy days.

Cold Dark Room

Alone in a cold dark room where I once
Lived my nightmares and could only dream
Sweet dreams
With no shoulder to cry on and
Nowhere to lean
I stand alone.
Just me.
Remembering.

Remembering a time when I felt that
No one loved me and no one cared.
They paid me no mind
And to the events of my life
They were completely blind.
They didn't know about this dark room
Where I lived my nightmares,
And all of the dangerous secrets that safely
lie within there.
And that I know of them all
I was a part of them all
I- was- a- victim -in -them –all
I – was – only-this-small.

I was seven and they didn't know
That he touched me.

He kissed me and licked me and roughly
fucked me.
They didn't know that she rammed three
fingers in me and made me bleed
Just to hear me scream.
And that he would want some too when he
came home from the penitentiary.
And he was trying to pay money to keep that
between him and me.
But he was the only one who attempted
unsuccessfully.

They didn't understand why
 I always stayed at my best friends house,
But I could always sleep sweet there.
No one touched me,
Only tucked me in and
Helped me say my prayers.
No one understood why I set the bed on fire
And poked a hole in the waterbed.
They didn't understand why
I'd rather sleep on the floor instead.
They didn't know about the cold dark room
Where I was living my nightmares.

No matter how beautifully decorated
This room will always be cold.

Full of dangerous secrets
That dare be told.
As I stand in this room remembering
That I could only dream sweet dreams
With no shoulder to cry on
And nowhere to lean
I stand alone.
Just me.
Remembering.

Remembering a time when I felt
It was me against the world.
I couldn't trust anyone.
I was the lone girl.
I stayed strapped and watched my back
No one else did.
I kept a piece to live in peace
Tired of living in fear.
Tired of crying unnecessary tears
I became fear.
And although you could still see
A glimpse of my good heart.
You can pinpoint where it began to separate
Where it began to fall apart.

In this cold dark room where I lived my
nightmares and

Dreams slowly began to not be so sweet
On the other side of that door
No one knew the things that were happening
to me.
They didn't know
Of the secrets that were being protected
They didn't know
That there were secrets being protected
Instead of a little girl
A little girl who grew to
Not trust anything about the world.

The Middle of a Love Story

We used to take long walks
And have lunch at the park
And have long talks.
Just looking into each other's eyes
Fulfilled that moments desires
You used to open my doors
And pull out my chairs
Chivalry isn't dead
It's all right there
You held my hand
Everywhere we went
Like you were showing everyone
Who you were with
You told me I was beautiful every single day
And you always made sure
There was a smile on my face
You taught me the difference
Between a relationship and a partnership
And showed that you would provide
Absolute perfect companionship
You used to look me in the eye
And tell me you couldn't live without me
And that you didn't have any doubts about
me

You never made plans that I wasn't included
in
And we shared everything
We even had the same friends.
You always noticed
When I changed my hair or my nails
And you would take me out dancing
And out for cocktails.
We shared a lot of experiences
Doing things together with no consequence.
We were reckless at times
But mostly played it safe.
Both of us knowing
There was a time and a place.

Always arguing and fighting
I couldn't take it anymore
I had to get out so I did
I just walked right out of the door.
Why I felt the need to leave?
Well I'm still unsure
But I wasn't looking back
And that I knew for sure
What I didn't know was
You'd keep calling me and writing me,
sending me e-mails
Sending me text messages

And voicemails to my cell
I didn't know you'd send my favorite flowers
Every day of the week.
And little notes with them saying
How I made you weak.
And I didn't know
That you'd continue to show up at my door
Asking for another chance
Offering everything I ever wanted and more

Notice that we always read about love
When it's in its prime or after it's reached its
peak
And the heartbreak it caused
And the feelings of defeat
But what about the time in between
When you question
If things are as they seem?
Like when you know you're in love
And you think it'll go far
But you're not just not quite ready
To open that jar.
When you talk about marriage
And one day having kids
But thinking about everything you want to do
Before you put in that bid.
When you're noticing things about each other

That you didn't notice before
And little things
Seem to begin irking you more and more.
What about when you stop wanting to share?
It's what you're accustomed to
Because both of you are always there.
And what about when you start thinking
About whether it's love, comfort or both
And you're trying to figure out
What feeling to host.
Yeah we only read about love
When it's in its prime
Or after it's reached its peak
And the heartbreak it caused
And feelings of defeat.
But what about the times in between?
Why do they always leave out
The middle of a love story?

His Hip Hop

She was his hip-hop.
The way she talked,
The way she dressed,
She even had hip-hop in the way she walked.
Indeed, she was his hip-hop.
She was so smooth
That's what he called her
He said that she was smooth.
The way she gazed into his eyes
Breaking all the rules
And keeping him hypnotized
Yeah she was smooth.
Especially in the way she spoke,
Wording her phrases so well
It took you through several phases.
The way she wrapped her words around her
voice
As she wrapped her voice around her words
She was hip-hop.

She was his hip-hop.
She always kept it intact
She was always fly
Every time he saw her
He thought, Me Oh My!

She always supplied him with
Treats for his eyes
And she gave his nose the gift
Of her sweet scent, she was it.
Indeed, she was his hip-hop.
Not a woman alive could strut in her pumps
Or even walk in her sneakers,
That's the kind of music that went
Roaring through his speakers
And on his tube, his very own
Fly girl who also had a clue
And she was gorgeous, splendid even
To him no one could compare
To the sight he was seeing.
He was seeing hip-hop
She was his hip-hop

With the walk of an undiscovered star
That captured his attention quickly
Making him want to follow her
No matter how far, and swiftly
The way her hips effortlessly swayed
From left to right
And how it seemed as though
She were floating every time she caught his
sight
And as she would approached him

He would watch her in awe thinking
She's my hip-hop she's my poetry in motion.
Indeed she was his hip-hop.
Wearing heels so high she felt like she could
Touch the sky…and she had legs for days…
Or so she made it seem
But it undeniably was all her
And it was all preposterously mean.
She walked to a beat
That he couldn't help but flow to
And the way her booty bounced with each
step
It seemed to be something
She couldn't help but move to.
She was hip-hop.

She was his hip-hop.
He felt good knowing that she knew
something
And when the time came
She would inspire him to do something.
She set the tones for his moods
Provided him with a nourishment
That you can't get from food.
Hip-hop is a friend that would never leave
And when he was in doubt
He would look to her for that Poetic Relief

That's what she was born to be.
His Hip-hop.

How It Seems

She was still a baby
But she seemed to be doing big girl things.
The future wasn't on her mind.
Or so it seemed.
Dressed like she just stepped out of a
magazine,
She was more fly than any girl
Who had ever been sixteen.
From the outside looking in
She looked as though she was in desperate
Need of a friend.
Always walking with her Head down,
She couldn't win for losing.
She was always the talk of the town.
Who was at home to take care of this young
girl?
Who is it not telling her that she is the future
of this world?
I mean she seemed loose
And her tongue always slipped slick
And she popped her gum
And walked with her hands on her hips.
Every time she was seen
It was with a different guy,
Her eyes bloodshot red

Like she just finished getting high.
She always had a pocket full of money
And no one ever knew where it came from
So they assumed that she did whatever she
could to make some.
She was the only girl in the hood
Really dressing like she was in Hollywood
And all the girls hated
Because they wish that they could.
She was friends with all of the drug dealers
And anyone else who was making money;
She seemed to be making her mark
So that she would never have to go hungry.
But of course people don't mind their
business
Yet they don't care enough to look carefully
Because things are not always
Exactly what they seem to be.

I am accustomed to nice things
And I keep my family first in my life.
These are just the things
I'm not willing to sacrifice.
Not only am I ready for what the world has to
offer,
I am going to pursue my dreams
Because I know they will take me farther.

I want to make a lot of money and live
lavishly.
I want extremely nice things.
And one day I want to settle down
And finally find my king.

I just lost my parents,
My whole world just died.
I can't go a day
Without letting loose my mournful cries.
Leaving my eyes bloodshot red
As I wished my parents were here
Or I too was dead.
My older brothers take care of me.
They don't have a clue what they're doing
But they know how to show love for me.
That's what they're proving
Never allowing me to go anywhere alone
They made it their business
To be my personal chaperones.
Knowing that people out there
They always point and stare.
They're always judging me
And I don't think it's fair.
But then again I don't really care
Because while they're out there
Focusing on who's on the scene

They're not smart enough to know
That things aren't always
As they seem.

Chapter 3

Archetypes of Love

A Mother's Love / Space / You Make Me Feel / Your Kiss / Best Enemy / Falling / This Can't Be Love

A Mother's Love

No matter how she loves you
She does it in a way that only she can
And it can't be substituted
Not ever,
By no man.
The way she takes care of you
Better than you would think to take care
yourself
Makes you want to reciprocate
So she gets to experience it for herself.
There is a bond there that can never be
broken
Even if you tried to do it yourself.
A bond greater than you'll ever have
With anyone else.

When you think about it
She truly is your very best friend
She'll always be there.
She'll be there through thick
She'll be there through thin
She'll be there to support you
Whether you lose or you win.
She's there when you need something
She's there when you need nothing at all

She's made a commitment to you
That no one else could ever live up to.

She was there to talk about that very first kiss
And when she asked how it was, you
blushed, a little.
But still you gave her a little dish.
She was there to help prepare for your first
date.
Giving you a curfew and the don'ts
And to tell you, you looked great.
She got you ready for homecoming
And prom night she made sure you had the
look of royalty
And she treated you as such
Putting you first and
Showing you a sincere loyalty.
And at graduation she had it all under control
All you did was show up and pose.
She got you ready for college
And for living on you own
And prepared you for the ways of the world
Although she would never leave you alone.

She put you on a path to success
You want to make her proud
So you do your very best.

You don't want to disappoint her
And you try your very best not to
But no matter what happens
She has an undying love for you.
Because that's a mother's love

Space

Space
A period of time, an empty place
The distance from others that a person needs
for comfort
A period of time, an empty place
The distance from others that a person needs
for comfort.

Comfort
Freedom from pain, trouble or anxiety
Freedom from pain, trouble or anxiety

Space
A period of time, an empty place
The distance from others that a person needs
for comfort
A period of time, an empty place
The distance from others that a person needs
for comfort

Comfort
Freedom from pain, trouble or anxiety
Freedom from pain, trouble or anxiety

Freedom
The quality or state of being free
Unrestricted use
Free…unrestricted use

I love when you invade my space.
It creates comfort.
A feeling of free…unrestricted use
My space becomes our space creating
freedom,
 Freedom from pain, trouble, or anxiety

You Make Me Feel

Just the thought of you
Makes me smile
It brings joy to my heart
Knowing you're worth my while
When I'm with you I can be myself
And that means more to me than anything
else
I cherish our moments
Of love laughter and fun
Nothing can break us down
Especially as we become one.

You make me feel so brand new
I can't imagine my life without you
I know that your love is true
I want to be with you and only you

What I'm trying to say is
That I love you
What I'm trying to get at is
That I need you
My pride used to get in the way
Of the things I had to say
It's not like that any more
Because now I'm completely sure

That it's you that I adore

You make me feel so brand new
I can't imagine nm life without you
I now that your love is true
I want to be with you and only you.

You're my heart, my soul
My love, my air
No matter what happens
I'll always be there
As a lending hand
Or a resting post
No matter the feeling
I'll be there to host
I love you
I know you love me too
That's why I put my trust in you
You make me happy
You make me feel so good
You excite me
Like only you could.

You make me feel so brand new
I can't imagine my life without you
I know that your love is true
I want to be with you and only you.

Your Kiss

Come grace me with the presence of your
lips upon mine.
When you kiss me I fall into a trance
And the feeling is so sublime.
You send my heart racing and
You put my soul at ease
And this is what happens
Each and every time you kiss me.
My body melts away
Along with my words
Your lips speak to me
Saying things I've never heard.

It's like you strategically place butterflies in
my stomach
And tickle my spine with a feather
Getting me excited from the inside out
As you indulge me in this simple but special
pleasure
Enticing my lips to your own
I enjoy the massage that you bestow upon
them
Such a magnificent feeling that you provide
I must part my lips to let you in

Loving the way you stroke my lips with your
tongue
Meeting mine in the center
I don't get cold
But my spine has its own private winter.
It's amazing the way you kiss me
Whether it's soft, playful or rough
Those lips were made for me
I can never get enough.
Luring me into your hold
You caress me and comfort me too
You're only thinking it but I part my lips and
say
"Did you feel that too?"

Best Enemy

You call yourself my best friend
If you're the best that friendship has to offer
I can do without it
Conversation over
I have nothing more to say about it

Except
How could you do that shit to me?
I always held you down
I know about everything
And I've never made a sound
I warned you about your outsiders
And randoms you kept around
Turns out you were one of them

Down
Until I wasn't anymore
My life kept moving forward
And you tried to block each door.
It's like you wanted me to
Crash, burn or
At the very least
Fall to the floor.
I'm done.

No I'm not
What the hell were you thinking?
Did these ideas come to you
When you were drinking?
Or was it when
You were with that bitch?
The destroyer of your relationships
Who never answers the phone when you need
to vent
And wouldn't answer the door if you needed
to take a shit
That's it.

No it ain't
You were never a friend to me
But I was damn sure one to you
Your parents didn't trust you
They could throw you too far
With me around
They didn't think they had to look to hard
And I was always your alibi
Whether with them or the law
I was your friend
But you were never mine
You betrayed me
Time after time
And then again after time.

I'm out.

Falling

You made me fall for you with no intentions
to catch me.
Still I attached to the discomfort I felt from
early.
Your we's turned to I's
And still I can't open my eyes.
Your we's turned to you's and still
I can't see how I'm being used.
Your appreciation turned expectation turned
nothing at all
And still
You're not there to catch me when I fall.
And still I do.
I fall
Into a mad trance over you
Not trusting in my heart or my mind
But in my flesh I do.
To be you and
Do what you do
Not to do much
Just feel me up
And fill me up.
My body constantly yearning for your touch
You feel me up and fill me up
With what my body needs so much

And I'm still falling
But I haven't hit the ground
And when I do
I suspect you won't be around

See I lured you to me
With no intentions to capture
I just wanted to play the captor
You know seductive but innocent
Wrap you up in my words
Make you think the world is yours
And then you'll give it to me.
All I had to do was smile at you
Flirt a little and
Tell you you're cute
I had your mind and your soul
So your body got shook
But you didn't know why
You didn't suspect me for a crook
You tried to play me
Thought I wouldn't catch on to the game
But I flipped it
That feeling that you're feeling
Is really ashamed.
You made me fall
With no intentions to catch me
So I tried to push you over the edge

This Can't Be Love

I love you, he says as I open my eyes
He's been watching me sleep
Come on I made breakfast
Get up. Let's go eat.
I stand and stretch
Before sliding my slippers on my feet
And as I pass the thermostat
I turn off the heat.
I continue to follow him to the table
And find my plate is already made
Good morning my love
This is how you'll start your wonderful day.
Pancakes, sausage and fresh fruit
My favorite
I take my time
I take small bites
Chewing slowly
I savor it.

I watch as he moves about carefree
As he sings along with The Temptations
Completely off key.
He pulls me up to dance
Totally offbeat
He has two left feet

And won't let me lead.
So dancing turns into a two-step and
The Bankhead bounce
Before we decided to just
Jump up and down
Then he twirls me
Around and around
And then dips me
Low to the ground
He picks me up slowly
After hearing a gasping sound.
As he pulled me up he gave me a box
Inside was a rock
Big enough to solve child hunger
Big enough to leave no wonder
I need another pancake.

Nice and full
He led me to the bathroom
A bubble bath awaited
And the fresh scent of vanilla filled the air
He undressed me slowly
And let down my hair
He took my hand
And I stepped in
He bathed me sensually
Me trembling every time

He touched my bare skin
He lathered me
Slowly, carefully
Slightly irritated by my constant flinch
Especially when approaching the bruises
They hurt like hell when the hot water hits
I'm sorry he says
As I begin to cry
Finally an apology
And he patted me dry
You do know this is all your fault right?
Just stop doing things that I don't like
Stop bringing out my urge to fight.
Blaming me for his actions
That just isn't right
And that's what finally
Brought out my urge to fight.
Late that night while he was sound asleep
I packed my bags
I didn't leave
I got a good night sleep.
I awakened first and got ready for my day
And made breakfast without delay
But he woke up late.
Revenge is a dish best served cold.
He was starving.
For every black eye

For every busted lip
He deserved to pay for this shit.
For every bump
And every bruise
He deserved to suffer however I choose.
For every broken bone
And every lost strand of hair
He deserved to be tortured
Beyond what he could bear.
He deserved to pay
With these thoughts I smiled
And slid him his plate.
He took a bite
And his eyes got wide
And he kneeled over in pain
And I took my leave
Without shame.

Chapter 4

This Chapter's About Sex

Last Night / Made The First Move / Heat Wave / Success Sex / Good Morning

Last Night

The look in your eyes
As you watched me just be.
You undressed me with your eyes
And then you undressed me.
Removing my shirt
You kissed each breast
And as you removed everything else
You kissed the rest.
With each kiss
Came a lick
You made me yearn for the dick.
When I finally stood naked
You admired my body
Before deciding to take it.
You lay me on the bed,
Straddling me
Keeping your hand behind my head
Allowing me to feel your dick grow
And harden in between my legs.
That was a measure of pleasure
No one else could fathom but me.
I wanted you in
Bu you just wouldn't let me win.
I nibbled on your ears
I licked on your neck

I sucked on your lips,
As I got nice and wet.
You bit my neck
You nibbled my nipples
You sucked my tits hard
And then soft with a little tickle
You licked my belly
Down to the center
And when your tongue pressed
My legs opened for you to enter.
You kiss me down my legs
And then back up
Then you stood up
You stepped back
Looking delicious
I wanted a suck.
You extended your hands for me to take
So I did
I didn't even think about it.
You stood me up and kissed me,
Sensually.
Then you gazed in my eyes
And smacked my ass.
I blushed with pleasant surprise.
My juices start flowing out
From inside.

I kiss up and down your body
As you did mine and
You moan with pleasure
Each and every time.
I kiss your lips hungrily
I want you quiet.
But when I grabbed your manhood
You just couldn't fight it.
You lift me
And kissed me
And I wrapped my legs around you
Quivering.
Slowly you lower me
Onto the bed
And trail your tongue down my body
Until your head was between my legs.
You delivered an unexpected sensation
Of timeless exhilaration
Ye my body still blazed
With anticipation.
Flipping me over
You flicker your tongue
Up and down my spine
It arched and you proceeded
To take me from behind
Ass up high.

You deliver slow deep strokes
Filling my walls
And with your quickening thrust
You slapped my clitoris with your balls.
You stopped abruptly and
Pulled your penis out
Shocked and appalled
I immediately begin to pout.
You flipped me over
And penetrated my vessels
With a deep thrust
Giving my body
An exhilarating rush
Without easing up.
Your body invaded my mind
Taking complete control
Keeping me in your stronghold
Until you felt me explode.
Forcefully my waves pulled you in
I remember you telling me that
You couldn't swim but
When you caught that wave
You perfected it
On a whim.

Interminable was the flow
And it flowed

Until I felt
A brush of air down below.
My eyes opened
My head sprang up
You pulled me up
Cupping my buttocks.
I wrapped my legs around you
And sat as you sat down
And as you squeezed my breast
I move back and forth
And around and round
As I catch my groove
I hopped up and down
Giving an erotic frown
As my juices trickled down.
Catching the waterfall
That you were chasing
Your body went crazy
And the feeling was amazing.
An award winning performance
And award winning endurance.
I couldn't take any more but
You gave a few more strokes
For assurance.
The last one made me weak
Still my body tightened around you
And my outcry

Prompted your sweet release.
Last night.

Made the first move

I watch him sit for a bit
Looking him up and down
I notice
There's something to be found.
There's a bulge in his slacks
But I'm not taken aback
Instead I'm in pursuit
Knowing what I want
But wondering what he'll do.
Will he hide?
Or oblige?
Will he run?
Or will he cum?
I decide to find out for myself
I don't need his help
Leading where I want him to follow,
I make small talk
When all I really want to do is
Pleasure him and
Leave him shocked
As he sits in his chair
I let down my hair
I remove my shirt
It had to go first
And as I step out of my pants

I perform a little dance
Moving nice and slow
He's watching me
Admiring me from head to toe
It's midday
So I can't stay
I have to have it
So I take it while he sits
I wondered about his reaction
And well this is it.
I climb aboard and immediately start
grinding
Back and forth, up and down
Around and around
While I remain sitting down.
Facing one another hungrily
We could not wait for this
Locking my legs as we lock eyes
We couldn't help but kiss.
Ecstasy in the air
He tugs my hair
And faster and faster
And faster I go
Until the moment when
We're ready to explode.

Heat Wave

Hot sticky wet
The humidity has made its way inside
The once open windows now closed
Only a ceiling fan spins slowly
The AC isn't broken
But it refuses to blow.
The house is spotless
It's cooler that way.
Especially on this miserably hot day
I lie atop my bed wearing
Only my bra and panties
I can't bear a t-shirt
The thought of any clothes
Makes my skin burst.
No need for light
The sun shines bright
Keep the shades drawn.
I walk around in search
Of a cooler room
And when I find one
You emerge and
Share in my doom.
These four walls
Even they look heated
The paint seems to be running

Then again I can't see clearly
It's not
I'm hallucinating
There's a heat wave.
Maybe.
Lying on our backs
In the middle of the floor
Closed windows
Drawn shades
And a closed room door
You realize you don't need
Your clothes anymore
They come off

Hot, sticky, wet
The dew between my neck and his lips
Cause us to temporarily stick.
It sends tingle down my spine
And around to my clit.
Now the heat
Has me I heat
Too hot to fight
You admit defeat.
I stick to your glow
With every kiss I bestow.
Your body is so soft
I can't keep my hands off.

Tick tock tick tock
It's so quiet
We can hear the ticking of the clock
Over our heavy breaths
Matching the rhythm of our rock
It's hot
But I don't want it to end
Because it's hot
Pulling out and thrusting in
A sure win.
Exuberantly having
The best sex yet
I'm impressed
This heat wave is
Hot, sticky, wet.

Success Sex

Success sex
You know right after completing the day's
quest
Sometimes before
But usually after
You wash off the day's sweat
Yes
I mean that sex
That makes you look forward
To the hard day's work tomorrow
Because you know that
Success sex will follow.

Good morning

I awakened not to your morning wood
But how I wish I would
Straddle you and ride
Like I've just caught
The morning tide.
Eyes of desire closed slight
As I catch my groove and take flight
I ride and ride
And ride and ride
Until you flip me over
And take me from behind.
Driving and strong and squeezing my breast
I awaken, panting
No longer at rest
Longing for your touch
You're not here but
I need it so much.
I didn't wake up to your morning wood
But my oh my
How I wish I would.

Chapter 5

This Here Life

Life's Pleasures / Just Blow It In The Sky /
Scars and Stripes / Tomorrow / Elements /
That Kind of Fun

Life's Pleasures

Sit back, relax and enjoy life's pleasures.
Just enjoy it young one,
If you know what I know, you better
Grab hold of all of its possibilities
And see which ones you can make your own
pleasant realities.
Live your dreams and chase your waterfalls.
Create stories for your children
Of great success and even of downfall.
Experience the love.
The love of family, of another and the love
for your craft.
Nothing else you experience will hold a torch
to that.
Take an adventure,
At the fork in the road, go left instead of
right.
You're looking for a little change
And down that road everything just might.
Do something to change the future of your
successors.
So big that they want to do something bigger
Or another contributing gesture
Try not to walk but stroll to enjoy the breeze.
Bask in the ambiance of nature's finest.

Set your mind free,
Let it stay at ease.

Sit back, relax and enjoy life's pleasures.
Live, love, laugh.
Live everyday as if it were your last.
Just love life and laugh.
Laugh every chance you get.
Don't let petty things get you upset.
Learn how to forgive and to forget.
Do your best, not to live with any regret.
Enjoying life's pleasures,
It is a test.

Sit back, relax and enjoy life's pleasures.
Create wonderful memories to share when
you get old,
And stories that have secret life lessons to
unfold.
Do something you thought you would never
do.
Just so you don't have to say
That you passed up the opportunity
When it was presented to you.
Laugh, cry, get angry and laugh again
Get angry, cry, laugh, and laugh some more
Live life the way you desire

It has so much to offer and so much in store.
Experience bumps in the roads
So you can share them with those after you
Not only that
Include they fun they brought too.
Because it's times like those
That create stories that your family will love
to listen to
When you get old
Try new things
You don't truly know what you like until
you've had it all
So do a little of this and a little of that
We don't have much time; we might as well
have a ball.

Sit back, relax and enjoy life's pleasures
Live, love, laugh
Live everyday as if it were your last
Just love life and laugh
Laugh every single chance you get
Don't let petty things get you upset
Learn how to forgive and forget
Do your best, not to live with regret.
Enjoying life's pleasures
It is a test

Just Blow It In The Sky

Allow the pressures of you day
To just blow away.
Watch them evaporate into thin air
Leaving you without those worries
Allowing you to no longer care.
Take a breath that calms your spirit
And frees your mind.
One that takes you to another place
Of a more mature kind.
Now let this breath be to help you relax,
Then the one that blocks further impact
And the breath of satisfaction
Comes right after that.

Take a deep breath
Hold it in
Then exhale
Just blow it in the sky.

Allow the tension to be released
From your mind, heart and body
The day is over
You're now experiencing your night
So enjoy it

Take a breath that puts away the urge to
fight.
Take a breath that feels like winter in your
lungs
Like a snowfall on a cold winter day.
Building snowmen and having snow fights
Remember the fun.
Inhale a breath of air that
Brings back childhood memories
Of laughter and peace.
A time where you could be reckless
And everything would still be fine
Take another breath that reminds you of that
time.
Let the next breath you take
Be one that brings you back home
And the one after that is to
Help you appreciate it and it alone
Now take this breath
That signifies you
Each breath you take
Makes you, you

Take a deep breath
Hold it in
Then exhale
Just blow it in the sky.

Scars and Stripes

To the untrained eye
These are stretch marks.
She was either small, and got big
Or the other way around
Either way they represent her current number
of pounds
But she was small
Got pregnant
Now she's small again
That baby did more than just
Stretch her skin
You call them stretch marks but they're not
That's Right!
They're Stripes!
Stripes she earned
Doing her term.
It didn't end when they cut her open to get
the baby out
Scared but happy that they got him safely out
Praying through her own survival
Because surgery like that
Can cause a problem arrival
Yes she earned her scars and stripes.

To the untrained eye

These are stretch marks
She was either big and got small
Or the other way around
Either way it represents
Her current number of pounds.
She was big and got small
And her confidence grew
As she saw the weight fall
Yes she deserves the hype
You call them stretch marks
But she earned those stripes.
Not knowing what to do with loose skin
Too embarrassed to ask a family member or
even best friend.
She got a tummy tuck
And she tried to keep it a secret
But after finding out it was a major surgery
she knew she'd never be able to keep it.
She was fighting for her life
While under the knife
She earned her scar and stripes

To the untrained eye
These are stretch marks
She was either small and got big
Or the other way around
Either way it represents

Her current number of pounds.
You really don't see anything
With an untrained eye
Especially if you can't see
That she earned
Her scar and stripes.

Tomorrow

Tomorrow comes every day
And waits patiently to be embraced.
Those who say that tomorrow never comes
Say it because they don't chase it
And for them
They're right
Their tomorrow will never come.
Tomorrow is the light at the end of the tunnel
It is what will be
Future, life
They very thing for which we fight.
Love, peace,
Life's desires and necessities.
Tomorrow is when we become
What we've always dreamed we'd be.
It's when we do
What we've always dreamed of doing
And it's when we become
The person we dream to be…the final me.

Tomorrow comes every day
Urging us to take a piece of it and
Longing for us to have more of it
But instead some of us just brush it off.
We just ignore it

Some people lock themselves into today
For fear of what tomorrow has in store
Because they have never had a dream
A piece of themselves they have to fight for.

Elements

The air
Life and death of me
My savage heart beats with
Strength, bravery, courage
Love you have my heart.
I dream about you at night
And I daydream about you.
Mind consuming
You must be knowledge
Palms itching with want
I will have you.
They say the heart wants
What the heart wants
Mine is savage.

The earth
It's how I live
It's where I live
They say home is where the heart is
I say it's where all my stuff is
The heart is home
Life revealed in its windows.
So the heart is home
Where I keep all that's mine
Any of worth.

And the secrets of life
Are scattered throughout the earth.

Water
We shouldn't live off of bread alone
If you think the grass is greener
On the other side
You should water your own.
Water is the answer to some questions
And the cure to many pains
Not enough
Yet plenty
Have a drink.

Wind
Blowing in my hair
My mind is blown
To see how fresh air can
Put your body in a different mode
Involuntary dance
As the wind controls my body
Rocking, swaying
A natural hottie.

Fire
Desire radiates from my thighs
Passion through my chest

Lava moisturizes my eyes
I breathe smoke
And I speak fire
I told you my heart was savage

That Kind Of Fun

I didn't stay for good morning but
That doesn't mean it wasn't one
Baby I had fun.

That mind blowing, juices flowing,
Toe curling, fist hurling kind of fun.
That If you never had a night like that
You better have you one fun
That ready for the world
Even after falling asleep to the sun fun.

I didn't stay for good morning but
That doesn't mean it wasn't one.
Baby I had fun.

Chapter 6

Ruthless Undomesticated Heart

It Costs / Feeling Some Kind Of Way / It's Complicated / He Thinks I'm Sexy / I Don't Love You / Over Before It Began / No White Horse

It Costs

I get money
You already know
I plant jewels motherfucker
And I reap what I sow.
I'm all woman
I'm fruitful and I multiply
I'm so great
I increase your supply.

I get money
'Cause I'm good at it.
I got that bag
Before someone else
Could come and snatch it.
I'm not hungry.
If I want to keep it that way
I gotta be up
To get that worm
Before these birds every day.
What can I say?
I'm the type that love to get paid
And at the end of the night
I'm the type that love to get laid
It's just my way.
I introduced you to some new shit

So well
You went out
Bought me a new whip
With matching kicks.

My house stay clean
But I'm no Merry Maid.
I'm a boss
So I call them up
When I need my bed made.
I eat good
I'm a good cook.
Not Martha Stewart
I'm Auntie Fe with it
I hear
Your new bitch feeding you
Noodles and Hi-C and shit

I'm a let you
See me be that bitch
But it's gon' cost
I'm a boss
I'm a let you
See me be that bitch
But its gon' cost
I'm a boss

Don't call me
Because your new bitch whack
And you miss the way
I did that thing way back.
Don't call me because
Your new bitch broke.
She can't count dollars
Don't make sense and
She's draining you slow.
Don't call me because
Your bitch can't cook
Not even from a book
I don't know how she got you hooked.
Your bitch can't even order out right.
All your meals are light.
You're hungry, no starving
Now you're looking for my ass to bite.
Don't call me because
That bitch lazy.
She gets bored and goes crazy
And she wants to have your baby.
Don't call me because
Your new bitch weak.
No book smarts, no street smarts
So her future looks bleak.
Don't call me because
Your bitch don't have no goals

Just sit and wait
For you to get home
No ambition to get her own.

Don't call me
Why are you calling me?
Please
Keep living your life
Where I can't se
Don't call me
Why are you calling?
How'd you get through?
I'm bossin'
First minutes free
You're on minute two.

I see
You want your baby with the bag back
The one
Who massaged you
And kept your back scratched.
Look at that at.
I bet
You miss
Playing in my hair and rubbing my scalp.
You miss
Pulling without pulling it out

I know
You miss my warm and loving touch
And how I stroked you ego
Just enough.
I think
You miss
Home cooked meals and
Late night desserts
And getting things started
Before I could first.
I got it
You miss your ride or die
With the unfair fight.
Whose bark doesn't compare to her bite.
I got it
You miss your trophy type
With the trophy life.
You thought I'd be there forever
Playing common law wife.

I'm a let you
See me be that bitch
But it's gon cost
I'm a boss, bitch
I'm a let you
See me be that bitch
But its gon cost

I'm a boss, bitch
Don't call me
Why are you calling me?
Please
Keep living your life
Where I can't see
Don't call me
Why are you calling?
How'd you get through?
I'm bossin'
First minute's free
You're on minute two

Feeling some kind of way

Well, no I didn't get butterflies
But I did get the overwhelming urge to smile
Umm, no, my heart didn't skip a beat.
It created a new one that made us both shift
in our seats
And tap our feet.
No I didn't have a bunch of thoughts
clouding my head
 I allowed him to provide me with something
to think about instead.
No, no, no shortness of breath,
 No trouble breathing.
None of those things
We enjoyed a wonderful evening
We had marvelous conversation
And a mini debate
He made me laugh a lot
Gave me a feeling I still can't shake.
Not one nervous bone in my body, not one
I was in my comfort zone
I felt at ease
I almost felt at home
That's when I knew I'd have to go

It's complicated

From time to time they get to look into each
other's eyes and genuinely say "I love you".

They kiss and make love unashamed.

Every once in a while they can get in a
conversation on the late night
Catching up on life
And disappearing into the daylight.

Sometimes they arrange to meet up for lunch.
Same day, same time, every month
The last time it was Thursday
The last Thursday in May.

There are times he surprise her with things
that make her smile.
Other times with things that let her know she
won't be seeing him for a while.
She sends him things back just to make him
think of her for more than a little while.
She sends it with the biggest smile.

When they can't take it anymore and just
want to hear one another's voice

They extend themselves to one another
beyond the available choice.

They've built a world all of their own
Their fairytale world so to speak
But still they were separated by two different
worlds
Neither of them really ready to take that leap.

They enjoy every bit of what they share
But neither of them feels the other is worth
more than what they have on their own
Real love can't be there
But they can't seem to just leave each other
alone
It's complicated

He Thinks I'm Sexy

T- Shirt and my panties on
My socks don't match
My hair is a mess
He couldn't care less
He thinks I'm sexy.

No bra on
My nipples are hard
Can be seen through my t shirt
He notices
He's ready to give them work

Just washed my face
And freshened my breath
My natural look
How he likes me best

Not primped and padded
And held a little too tight
But the look revealed
When my hair comes down
And my clothes fall off
At the end of the night
He thinks I'm sexy

I Don't Love You

I like spending all of my time with you
But I want to go home
I love my space too
I don't love you.

The sex is good and
I enjoy your morning wood but
I don't love you.

You're funny and
You always make me laugh
You're cool enough to chill with
And watch the time pass but
I don't love you.

I like kissing you in public
To make others jealous and
Turning down offers from your fellas but
I don't love you.

I could but I don't and
Even with time I wont
I don't love you.

Over Before It Began

He met her before his time
She was the woman he wanted
When it was all said and done
But for right now
He wanted to finish having his fun
Still he chose her
Knowing she wasn't truly the one
Also knowing
She'd let him know
When she was done

For him it was time to
Chase skirts and get money
Paint the town blue
Every night
With a different "you know who"
It was his time to
Stay fresh to death
And pursue nothing with depth

He was fun and all
And fun was all.
Just the way she liked him.
She wanted fun

Tired of serious relationships
Tired of searching for the one
She just wanted
The splendor of the moment
And every time she got
She owned it.
Soon being together
Seemed like more than fun was involved
He wasn't ready
She didn't want it
They agreed to separate
They just kept it one hundred.

No White Horse

Fuck that white horse bullshit
You tryna spit.
Pardon my French but
I'm a real bitch

I don't need to be saved
I have my own shining armor
I have a long shiny sword
Already the Queen of my castle
Don't take me to yours

There's no dungeon to save me from
I'm not locked in a tower
Not asleep awaiting your kiss to live
You don't have that power

No daddy issues or wicked stepmother
No psychological issues
To work through
No matter what fairytales
Have laid out for you

Don't burst through my door
With your boys playing trumpets behind you
This isn't band practice

Need I remind you?

Don't stop at my door
Doing a wheelie on a horse.
You won't be kissing me without permission
Or climbing my hair
To force a loving submission

I'm a Queen
I don't need saving
But you may want to save yourself
From me baby

I'm a warrior
And I happen to be Queen
So bow down proper
Before I get mean

Does it look like I need to be saved?
Do I look that well behaved?
I have my own transportation
Keep your white horse please
I have no need for your carriage
Or your noble steed.

www.ingramcontent.com/pod-product-compliance
Lightning Source LLC
Chambersburg PA
CBHW060356050426
42449CB00009B/1765